The Number
Cheesecake
Cookbook

Perfect Cheesecake Recipes That Even
Beginners Can Make

BY

MOLLY MILLS

License Notes

No part of this book may be copied, replicated, distributed, sold or shared without the express and written consent of the Author.

The ideas expressed in the book are for entertainment purposes. The Reader assumes all risk when following any guidelines and the Author accepts no responsibility if damages occur due to actions taken by the Reader.

An Amazing Offer for Buying My Book!

Thank you very much for purchasing my books! As a token of my appreciation, I would like to extend an amazing offer to you! When you have subscribed with your e-mail address, you will have the opportunity to get free and discounted e-books that will show up in your inbox daily. You will also receive reminders before an offer expires so you never miss out. With just little effort on your part, you will have access to the newest and most informative books at your fingertips. This is all part of the VIP treatment when you subscribe below.

SIGN ME UP: *https://molly.gr8.com*

Table of Contents

Cheesecake Recipes

AAAAAAAAAAAAAAAAAAAAAAAAAAAAAAAAAAAAAAAAAAAAA

Recipe 1: No Bake Cheesecake

This is an easy cheesecake recipe for those who don't want to be bothered with actually baking a cheesecake. I guarantee that everybody who tries a piece of this delicious cheesecake will be begging for more.

Yield: 12 Servings

Cooking Time: 1 Day and 45 Minutes

List of Ingredients:

- 1 ½ Cups of Graham Crackers, Crumbs Only
- 1/3 Cup of Brown Sugar, Light and Packed
- ½ teaspoons of Cinnamon, Ground
- 1/3 Cup of Butter, Soft and Melted
- 2 Packs of Cream Cheese, Soft
- 2 teaspoons of Lemon Juice, Fresh
- 1 Pint of Whipping Cream, Heavy Variety
- 1/3 Cup of Sugar, White
- 1 Can of Cherry Pie, Filling Only

AAAAAAAAAAAAAAAAAAAAAAAAAAAAAAAAAAAAAAAAAAAAA

Instructions:

1. Using a small sized bowl, mix together your first 3 ingredients together. Add in your melted butter and stir thoroughly to evenly combine. Press this mixture into a medium to large sized spring form pan and place into your fridge. Chill until firm to the touch.

2. Using another medium sized bowl, beat together your cream cheese and fresh lemon juice with an electric mixer until smooth in consistency. Add in your heavy whipping cream and sugar, making sure that you continue to beat until smooth in consistency and stiff to the touch.

3. Pour this cheesecake batter into your firm cheesecake crust. Top your cheesecake with your cherry pie filling.

4. Place your cheesecake back into your fridge and chill overnight. Serve whenever you are ready. Enjoy!

Recipe 2: New York Style Cheesecake

If you are looking to prepare a traditional cheesecake that you will fall in love with, this is the perfect recipe for you. This recipe is easy to make and tastes so delicious that I know you are going to want to make this dish over and over again.

Yield: 12 Servings

Cooking Time: 7 Hours and 30 Minutes

List of Ingredients:

- 15 Graham Crackers, Crumbs and Crushed
- 2 Tablespoons of Butter, Soft
- 4 Packs of Cream Cheese, Soft
- 1 ½ Cups of Sugar, White
- ¾ Cup of Milk
- 4 Eggs, Large in Size and Beaten
- 1 Cup of Sour Cream
- 1 tablespoon of Vanilla, Pure
- ¼ Cup of Flour, All Purpose Variety

AAAAAAAAAAAAAAAAAAAAAAAAAAAAAAAAAAAAAAAAAAAAA

Instructions:

1. The first thing that you will want to do is preheat your oven to 350 degrees. While your oven begins to heat up generously grease a medium to large sized spring form pan with a generous amount of cooking spray.

2. Then take a medium sized bowl and combine your graham crackers and soft butter together and mix thoroughly until mixed extremely well. Press this mixture into your greased spring form pan.

3. Next use a large sized bowl beat your cream cheese and sugar together with an electric mixer on the highest setting until light and fluffy in texture. Then combine your remaining ingredients together and continue to mix until your mixture is smooth in consistency.

4. Pour this newly formed batter into your spring form pan.

5. Bake your cheesecake pan into your oven to bake for the next hour, making sure that you do not overbake your cheesecake. After this time turn off your oven and let your cheesecake cool in your oven for the next 5 to 6 hours.

6. After this time remove from oven and place into your fridge to chill for an hour or so before serving. Enjoy!

Recipe 3: Classic Pumpkin Cheesecake

This is a classic and traditional cheesecake recipe that I know you won't be able to resist making yourself. While I know at first glance this will look like a tough recipe to prepare, don't be worried. It is actually quite easy to make and well worth the effort that you put in.

Yield: 12 Servings

Cooking Time: 1 Hour and 20 Minutes

List of Ingredients:

- ¾ Cup of Graham Crackers, Crumbs Only
- ½ Cup of Pecans, Ground
- 2 Tablespoons of Sugar, White
- 2 Tablespoons of Brown Sugar, Light and Packed
- ¼ Cup of Butter, Soft
- ¾ Cup of Sugar, White
- ¾ Cup of Pumpkin, Canned
- 3 Eggs, Yolk Only
- 1 ½ teaspoons of Cinnamon, Ground
- ½ teaspoons of Mace, Ground
- ½ teaspoons of Ginger, Ground
- ¼ teaspoons of Salt
- 3 Packs of Cream Cheese, Soft
- 3/8 Cup of Sugar, White
- 1 Egg, Large in Size and Beaten
- 1 Egg, Yolk Only
- 2 Tablespoons of Whipping Cream, Your Favorite Kind
- 1 tablespoon of Cornstarch
- ½ teaspoons of Vanilla, Pure
- ½ teaspoons of Lemon, Extract Only

AA

Instructions:

1. The first thing that you will want to do is preheat your oven to 350 degrees.

2. While your oven is heating up take your first 5 ingredients together and mix thoroughly until mixed extremely well. Press this mixture into a medium sized spring form pan.

3. Then combine your next 7 ingredients together in a medium sized mixing bowl. Mix vigorously until thoroughly combined.

4. Next beat your cream cheese with an electric mixer on the highest setting until light and fluffy in texture. While you are beating your cream cheese add in your sugar slowly and continue to beat.

5. Add in your remaining ingredients, continuously beating and mixing until your mixture is smooth in consistency.

6. Pour this newly formed batter into your spring form pan.

7. Bake your cheesecake pan into your oven to bake for the next 50 to 55 minutes. Make sure that you do not overbake your cheesecake. Remove from oven and cool for at least a couple of minutes before transferring to a wire rack to cool completely.

8. After your cheesecake has cooled place it into your fridge to chill and serve whenever you are ready. Enjoy!

Recipe 4: Rhubarb Style Cheesecake

This is a perfect cheesecake to make if you are looking to make a more exquisite dessert for your friends and family. With the sour cream topping this is one cheesecake dish that you are going to want to make nearly every day.

Yield: 12 Servings

Cooking Time: 1 Hour and 5 Minutes

List of Ingredients:

- 1 Cup of Flour, All Purpose Variety
- ¼ Cup of Sugar, White
- ½ Cup of Butter, Soft and Melted
- 3 Cups of Rhubarb, Finely Chopped
- ½ Cup of Sugar, White
- 1 tablespoon of Flour, All Purpose Variety
- 2 Packs of Cream Cheese, Soft
- ½ Cup of Sugar, White
- 2 Eggs, Large in Size and Beaten
- 1 Cup of Sour Cream
- 2 Tablespoons of Sugar, White
- 1 teaspoon of Vanilla, Pure

AA

Instructions:

1. The first thing that you will want to do is preheat your oven to 375 degrees. While your oven begins to heat up generously grease a medium to large sized spring form pan with a generous amount of cooking spray.

2. Take your first 3 ingredients together and mix thoroughly until mixed extremely well. You want to mix it together until your mixture is crumbly in texture. Press this mixture into your greased spring form pan.

3. Using a medium sized bowl mix together your next 3 ingredients until thoroughly mixed. Pour this mixture into your curst.

4. Place into your oven to bake for at least 15 minutes. After this time remove from oven and set aside for later use. Then reduce the temperature of your oven to 350 degrees.

5. Take out a large sized bowl and beat your cream cheese and sugar together with an electric mixer on the highest setting until light and fluffy in texture. Add in your eggs next and continue mixing until your mixture is smooth in consistency. Pour this over your rhubarb mixture.

6. Place back into your oven and bake for an additional 30 minutes or until fully firm. Make sure that you do not overbake your cheesecake. Remove from oven and set aside to cool.

7. Once your cheesecake is baking, make your topping by mixing together your remaining ingredients in a small sized bowl and stir to thoroughly combine. Once mixed well, pour on top of your hot cheesecake.

8. Serve your cheesecake whenever you are ready.

Recipe 5: Praline Style Cheesecake

This is a creamy style cheesecake that is packed full of rich and nutty butterscotch, making it a tasty treat to enjoy any time. I highly recommend that you serve a slice of this cheesecake with a dallop of your favorite whipped topping and a garnish of a few pecans to get the tastiest result with this recipe.

Yield: 12 Servings

Cooking Time: 1 Hour and 30 Minutes

Ingredients for Your Crust:

- ¼ Cup of Butter, Soft
- 1 Cup of Graham Crackers, Crumbs Only
- 3 Tablespoons of Brown Sugar, Light and Packed
- 1/3 Cup of Pecans, Finely Chopped

Ingredients for Your Filling:

- 2 Packs of Cream Cheese, Soft
- 1 ¼ Cup of Brown Sugar, Light and Packed
- 3 Eggs, Large in Size and Beaten
- 1 teaspoon of Rum Flavor, Extract
- 1 teaspoon of Vanilla, Pure
- ¼ Cup of Sour Cream
- 1/3 Cup of Pecans, Finely Chopped

Ingredients for Your Topping:

- 1 ½ Cups of Sour Cream
- ¼ Cup of Brown Sugar, Light and Packed
- ¾ teaspoons of Maple Flavor, Extract Only
- ½ teaspoons of Rum Flavor, Extract Only

AAAAAAAAAAAAAAAAAAAAAAAAAAAAAAAAAAAAAAAAAAAAA

Instructions:

1. The first thing that you have to do is make your crust. To do this melt your soft butter in a small sized saucepan. Once melted add in your graham cracker crumbs and your next 2 ingredients. Stir to evenly combine. Remove from heat and packed this mixture into the bottom of your medium sized spring form pan.

2. Next make your filling. To do this beat your light and packed brown sugar and soft cream cheese together using an electric mixer until smooth and fluffy in consistency. Then add in your next 5 ingredients and mix vigorously until thoroughly combined.

3. Pour this newly formed batter into your spring form pan.

4. Bake your cheesecake pan into preheated oven at 350 degrees to bake for the next 50 minutes to an hour or until your cheesecake is fully set. Make sure that you do not overbake your cheesecake. Remove from oven and cool for at least a couple of minutes before transferring to a wire rack to cool completely.

5. While your cheesecake is cooling, make your topping. To do this combine your remaining ingredients together in a small sized bowl and stir thoroughly until evenly mixed. Spread this mixture on top of your cheesecake and place back into your oven.

6. Bake for an additional 10 minutes. After this time remove your cheesecake from your oven and allow to cool.

7. After your cheesecake has cooled place it into your fridge to chill and serve whenever you are ready. Enjoy!

Recipe 6: Cookie Dough Cheesecake

If you are a fan of chocolate chip cookie dough ice cream, then I know you are going to love this cheesecake recipe. Even after trying a small piece of this cheesecake, I know you are going to be craving for more.

Yield: 12 Servings

Total Pre Time: 5 Hours and 20 Minutes

Ingredients for Your Crust:

- 1 ½ Cups of Wafers, Chocolate Flavored and Finely Crushed
- 2 Tablespoons of Sugar, White
- ¼ Cup of Butter, Soft and Melted

Ingredients for Your Cake:

- 2 Packs of Cream Cheese, Cut Into Small Chunks
- ¾ Cups of Sugar, White
- 2 tablespoons of Sugar, White
- 1 Cup of Sour Cream
- 3 Eggs, Large in Size and Beaten
- 1 teaspoon of Vanilla, Pure

Ingredients for Your Cookie Dough:

- ¼ Cup of Butter, Soft and Melted
- ¼ Cup of Brown Sugar, Light and Packed
- ¼ Cup of Sugar, White
- 2 Tablespoons of Water
- 1 teaspoon of Vanilla, Pure
- 1 Cup of Chocolate Chips, Semisweet Variety
- ½ Cups of Flour, All Purpose Variety

Ingredients for Your Topping:

- 1 Cup of Sour Cream
- 2 teaspoons of Sugar, White
- 1 teaspoon of Vanilla, Pure

AAAAAAAAAAAAAAAAAAAAAAAAAAAAAAAAAAAAAAAAAAAAA

Instructions:

1. The first thing that you will want to do is preheat your oven to 350 degrees. While your oven begins to heat up generously grease a medium to large sized spring form pan with a generous amount of cooking spray.

2. Take your first 3 ingredients together and mix thoroughly until mixed extremely well. Press this mixture into your greased spring form pan. Place your crust into your oven and bake for the next 8 hours. After this time remove from oven and set aside.

3. Next beat your cream cheese and at least 2 tablespoons of sugar with an electric mixer on the highest setting until fluffy and creamy in consistency. Next add in your remaining ingredients for your cake into your mixer and beat until thoroughly combined. Once smooth in consistency pour batter into your pre baked crust.

4. Next combine all of your ingredients for your cookie dough in a large sized bowl until evenly combined. Once combined drop your cookie dough onto your cake batter by the tablespoon, making sure that you push the dough beneath the surface of your cakes.

5. Bake your cheesecake pan into your oven to bake for the next 40 minutes. Make sure that you do not overbake your cheesecake. Remove from oven and cool on a wire rack to cool completely.

6. While your cheesecake is baking make your topping. To do so mix all of your ingredients together in a medium sized bowl and until evenly combined. Once mixed pour this mixture over your hot cheesecake once it comes out of the oven and allow your cake to cool to room temp before transferring to your fridge to chill for at least 4 hours.

Recipe 7: Sour Cream Style Cheesecake

This is a very easy cheesecake recipe to make. Not only is this cheesecake extremely delicious and incredibly filling. For the tastiest results I highly recommend topping a slice of this cake with some fruit topping and your favorite kind of whipped topping.

Yield: 12 Servings

Cooking Time: 1 Hour and 30 Minutes

List of Ingredients:

- 1 Shortbread Pie Crust, Medium in Size and Fully Prepared
- 2 Packs of Cream Cheese, Soft
- 1 Cup of Sugar, White
- 2 Eggs, Large in Size and Beaten
- 2 teaspoons of Vanilla, Pure
- 1 Cup of Sour Cream

AAAAAAAAAAAAAAAAAAAAAAAAAAAAAAAAAAAAAAAAAAAAAAAA

Instructions:

1. The first thing that you have to do is preheat your oven to 325 degrees.

2. While your oven is heating up, mix together all of your ingredients except for your prepared pie crust and mix thoroughly until creamy and smooth in consistency.

3. Add this filling into your shortbread pie crust.

4. Bake your cheesecake pan into preheated oven for the next hour to an hour and 10 minutes or until your cheesecake is fully set. Make sure that you do not overbake your cheesecake. Remove from oven and cool for at least a couple of minutes before transferring to a wire rack to cool completely.

5. After your cheesecake has cooled place it into your fridge to chill and serve whenever you are ready. Enjoy!

Recipe 8: Banana Split Cheesecake

Here is yet another cheesecake recipe that I know you are going to love simply because you don't have to bake it. It is also incredibly delicious, making you want to enjoy this tasty dish as often as possible.

Yield: 18 Servings

Cooking Time: 35 Minutes

List of Ingredients:

- 2 ½ Cups of Graham Cracker, Crumbs Only
- ¾ Cup of Butter, Soft and Melted
- 4 Cups of Confectioner's Sugar
- 2 packs of Cream Cheese, Soft
- 1 Can of Pineapple, Crushed and Drained
- 3 Bananas, Medium in Size and Cut into Quarters
- 1 Container of Whipped Topping, Frozen and Thawed
- 8 Cherries, Maraschino Variety and Cut into Halves
- ¼ Cup of Chocolate Syrup
- ½ Cup of Pecans, Cut Into Halves

AAA

Instructions:

1. The first thing that you want to do is blend your butter and graham cracker crumbs together until evenly combined together. Press this mixture into a medium to large sized spring form pan.

2. Then blend together your cream cheese and confectioner's sugar until smooth in consistency. Spread this mixture over your crust.

3. Then place your remaining ingredients in the following layers: pineapple, bananas, whipped topping, cherry halves.

4. Last Garnish with chocolate syrup and halved pecans.

5. Place your cheesecake into your fridge to chill for at least 8 hours. Serve whenever you are ready.

Recipe 9: Traditional German Cheesecake

If you are looking to enjoy a traditional and authentic German style cheesecake without going through of all of the hassle to do so, this is the recipe for you. It is relatively easy to put together and will leave you wanting more.

Yield: 12 Servings

Cooking Time: 7 Hours and 30 Minutes

List of Ingredients:

- 1 ½ Cups of Sugar, White
- 2 Tablespoons of Cornstarch
- 3 Tablespoons of Flour, All Purpose Variety
- 2 Packs of Cream Cheese, Soft
- 1 Pound of Cottage Cheese, Small in Size and Curd Style
- ½ Cup of Butter, Soft
- 4 Eggs, Medium in Size and Beaten
- 1 ½ Tablespoons of Lemon Juice, Fresh
- 1 teaspoon of Vanilla, Pure

AA

Instructions:

1. The first thing that you will want to do is preheat your oven to 350 degrees. While your oven is heating up generously grease a medium sized spring form pan.

2. Then mix together your next 3 ingredients together in a medium sized pan until thoroughly mixed.

3. Next beat your cream cheese and cottage cheese with an electric mixer on the highest setting until light and fluffy in texture. Then add in your remaining ingredients together, making sure that you mix vigorously until thoroughly combined.

4. Pour this newly formed batter into your spring form pan.

5. Bake your cheesecake pan into your oven to bake for 1 hour and 10 minutes. Make sure that you do not overbake your cheesecake. After this time turn off your oven and allow your cheesecake to sit in your hot oven for at least 2 more hours.

6. After this time remove from oven and cool for at least a couple of minutes before transferring to a wire rack to cool completely.

7. After your cheesecake has cooled place it into your fridge to chill for the next 4 hours and serve whenever you are ready. Enjoy!

Recipe 10: Oreo Cheesecake

This is a great cheesecake dessert dish that you can make without that much effort needed. I guarantee that once your friends and family try this dish for themselves, they won't be able to get enough of it.

Yield: 12 Servings

Cooking Time: 4 Hours and 5 Minutes

List of Ingredients:

- 24 Oreo Cookies, Evenly Divided
- 3 Tablespoons of Butter, Soft and Melt
- 3 Packs of Cream Cheese, Soft
- ¾ Cup of Sugar
- 1 teaspoon of Vanilla, Pure
- 3 Eggs, Large in Size and Beaten

AAAAAAAAAAAAAAAAAAAAAAAAAAAAAAAAAAAAAAAAAAAAA

Instructions:

1. The first thing that you will want to do is preheat your oven to 350 degrees. While your oven is heating up generously grease a medium sized spring form pan.

2. Then place your Oreo cookies into a Ziploc bag. Once sealed use a rolling pin and finely crush your cookies. Place your cookie crumbs into a medium sized bowl and mix with your soft butter. Mix well to combine and press this mixture into your spring form pan.

3. Next raise the heat of your oven to 425 degrees.

4. Then using a food processor or blender, add in your next 4 ingredients and process on the highest setting for a couple of seconds or until your mixture is smooth in consistency.

5. Add in your remaining ingredients and puree again until evenly combined and smooth in consistency.

6. Pour this mixture into your prebaked cheesecake crust. Top off with some of your Oreo cookies

7. Bake your cheesecake pan into your oven to bake for the next 45 minutes or until your cheesecake is firm. After this time remove your cheesecake from your oven and place onto a wire cooling rack to cool completely. Cover and store in your fridge to chill overnight until you serve it.

Recipe 11: Delicious Caramel Macchiato Cheesecake

Caramel Macchiato happens to be one of my favorite coffee drinks so what is better than mixing together a tasty coffee drink and a delicious treat such as a cheesecake? This cheesecake dish is so tasty, I know that you are going to love it.

Yield: 12 Servings

Cooking Time: 10 Hours and 3 Minutes

List of Ingredients:

- 2 Cups of Graham Crackers, Crumbs Only
- ½ Cup of Butter, Soft
- 2 Tablespoons of Sugar, White
- 3 Packs of Cream Cheese, Soft
- 1 Cup of Sugar, White
- 3 Eggs, Large in Size and Beaten
- 1 Container of Sour Cream
- ¼ Cup of Coffee, Strong and Brewed
- 2 teaspoons of Vanilla, Pure
- Some Whipped Cream
- Ice Cream, Caramel Flavor and For Topping

AAAAAAAAAAAAAAAAAAAAAAAAAAAAAAAAAAAAAAAAAAAAA

Instructions:

1. The first thing that you will want to do is preheat your oven to 350 degrees. While your oven is heating up generously grease a medium to large sized spring form pan.

2. Then mix together your next 3 ingredients together in a medium sized bowl until thoroughly mixed together. Press this mixture into the bottom of your greased spring form pan.

3. Place this crust into your oven to bake for at least 8 minutes. After that time remove it from your oven and set out to cool on a wire cooling rack.

4. Then reduce the heat of your oven to 325 degrees.

5. Next beat your cream cheese with an electric mixer on the highest setting until light and fluffy in texture. Then add in your remaining ingredients together, making sure that you mix vigorously until thoroughly combined.

6. Pour this newly formed batter into your prebaked cheesecake crust.

7. Bake your cheesecake pan into your oven to bake for 1 hour and 5 minutes. Make sure that you do not overbake your cheesecake. After this time turn off your oven and allow your cheesecake to sit in your hot oven for at least 15 minutes.

8. After this time remove from oven and cool for at least a couple of minutes before transferring to a wire rack to cool completely.

9. After your cheesecake has cooled place it into your fridge to chill for the next 8 hours and serve whenever you are ready. When serving garnish with your caramel sauce and whipped cream for the tastiest results.

Recipe 12: Nutella Cheesecake

Who doesn't love Nutella? If you are a huge fan of Nutella, then I know you are going to love this cheesecake recipe. It is packed full of chocolatey goodness and nutty peanut butter taste that you are going to want to make over and over again.

Yield: 8 Servings

Cooking Time: 4 Hours and 10 Minutes

List of Ingredients:

- 2 Packs of Cream Cheese, Soft and Warm
- ½ Cup of Sugar, White
- 1 Jar of Nutella
- ¼ teaspoons of Vanilla, Pure
- 1 Premade Crust, Graham Cracked Variety

AAAAAAAAAAAAAAAAAAAAAAAAAAAAAAAAAAAAAAAAAAAAA

Instructions:

1. Use a large sized bowl and add in your soft cream cheese and your sugar. Use an electric mixer and beat vigorously until smooth in consistency.

2. Add in your Nutella and pure vanilla and continue mixing until evenly mixed together.

3. Pour this mixture into your crust.

4. Cover and place into your refrigerator to chill for at least 4 hours. Serve whenever you are ready.

Recipe 13: Decadent Chocolate Cheesecake

This is a great cheesecake recipe to put together for nearly any special occasion. These is a rich tasting cheesecake that is packed full of chocolate flavor. I promise you that any chocoholic out there is just going to fawn over this recipe.

Yield: 12 Servings

Cooking Time: 1 Hour and 20 Minutes

List of Ingredients:

- 1 Cup of Cookies, Chocolate Variety and Crushed
- ¼ Cup of Butter, Soft
- 2 Tablespoons of Sugar, White
- ¼ teaspoons of Cocoa Powder, Unsweetened
- 3 Packs of Cream Cheese, Soft
- 1 Cup of Sugar, White
- 3 Eggs, Large in Size and Beaten
- ½ Pound of Chocolate Chips, Semisweet Variety
- 2 Tablespoons of Heavy Cream
- 1 Cup of Sour Cream
- Dash of Salt
- ¾ Cup of Irish Beer, Guinness Preferable
- 2 teaspoons of Vanilla, Pure
- 1 Square of Chocolate, Semisweet Variety

AAAAAAAAAAAAAAAAAAAAAAAAAAAAAAAAAAAAAAAAAAAA

Instructions:

1. The first thing that you will want to do is preheat your oven to 350 degrees. While your oven begins to heat up generously grease a medium to large sized spring form pan with a generous amount of cooking spray.

2. Take your first 4 ingredients together and mix thoroughly until mixed extremely well. Press this mixture into your greased spring form pan.

3. Next beat your cream cheese with an electric mixer on the highest setting until light and fluffy in texture. While you are beating your cream cheese add in your sugar slowly and continue to beat followed by your eggs. Continue to mix until your mixture is smooth in consistency.

4. Next combine your semisweet chocolate chips and heavy cream together in a small sized microwave bowl. Place into your microwave and cook until your chocolate is fully melted, making sure that you stir your mixture every 30 seconds or so.

5. Place your melted chocolate into a medium sized bowl and combine with your remaining ingredients, continuously beating and mixing until your mixture is smooth in consistency.

6. Pour this newly formed batter into your spring form pan.

7. Bake your cheesecake pan into your oven to bake for the next 45 minutes. Make sure that you do not overbake your cheesecake. Remove from oven and cool for at least an additional 45 minutes before transferring to a wire rack to cool completely.

8. After your cheesecake has cooled place it into your fridge to chill for the next 4 hours.

9. While your cheesecake is cooling, melt your remaining chocolate in your microwave until fully melted. Drizzle this mixture over your chilled cheesecake and serve whenever you are ready. Enjoy!

Recipe 14: Chocolate Fudge Truffle

Cheesecake

This is a cheesecake dish that I know every chocoholic out there will love. It is also extremely versatile, giving you the added benefit to make this dish in any kind of way you want. For the tastiest results I highly recommend drizzling some melted chocolate truffles over the top of it. Regardless of what you do I know you are going to love it.

Yield: 14 Servings

Cooking Time: 5 Hours

List of Ingredients:

- 1 ½ Cups of Wafers, Vanilla Flavored and Crushed Into Crumbs
- ½ Cup of Confectioner's Sugar
- 1/3 Cup of Cocoa Powder, Unsweetened
- 1/3 Cup of Butter, Soft and Melted
- 2 Cups of Chocolate Chips, Semi Sweet Variety
- 3 Packs of Cream Cheese, Cooled To Room Temp.
- 1 Can of Milk, Sweetened and Condensed
- 4 Eggs, Large in Size and Beaten
- 2 teaspoons of Vanilla, Pure

ΛΛΛΛΛΛΛΛΛΛΛΛΛΛΛΛΛΛΛΛΛΛΛΛΛΛΛΛΛΛΛΛΛΛΛΛΛΛΛΛΛΛΛΛΛΛΛΛ

Instructions:

1. The first thing that you will want to do is preheat your oven to 300 degrees. While your oven is heating up generously grease a medium sized spring form pan.

2. Then use a medium sized bowl and mix your first 4 ingredients together until thoroughly mixed. Press this mixture into the bottom of your greased spring form pan.

3. Next using the top of a double broiler, melt your chocolate chips until they are completely melted and smooth in consistency.

4. Next using a large sized bowl, beat your cream cheese vigorously with an electric mixer until smooth in consistency. Add in your remaining ingredients into your cream cheese and continue beating with an electric mixer until your mixture is smooth in consistency.

5. Pour this mixture into your prebaked cheesecake crust.

6. Bake your cheesecake pan into your oven to bake for the next 55 minutes or until your cheesecake is firm. After this time remove your cheesecake from your oven and place onto a wire cooling rack to cool. Once cooled, cover and place into your fridge to chill for a couple of hours. Enjoy whenever you are ready.

Recipe 15: Classic Key Lime Cheesecake

If you haven't had the chance to try key lime pie for yourself, then this cheesecake recipe is the perfect recipe to try to get you used to the taste. For the tastiest and most appealing results add a drop of green food coloring and garnish this cheesecake with some whipped cream.

Yield: 12 Servings

Cooking Time: 1 Hour and 30 Minutes

List of Ingredients:

- 1 ½ Cups of Graham Crackers, Crumbs Only and Ground
- 2 Tablespoons of Sugar, White
- ¼ Cup of Butter, Unsalted Variety and Melted
- 1 ¼ Pounds of Cream Cheese, Soft
- ¾ Cup of Sugar, White
- 1 Cup of Sour Cream
- 3 Tablespoons of Flour, All Purpose Variety
- 3 Eggs, Large in Size and Beaten
- ¾ Cup of Key Lime, Fresh and Juice Only
- 1 teaspoon of Vanilla, Pure

AAAAAAAAAAAAAAAAAAAAAAAAAAAAAAAAAAAAAAAAAAAAAA

Instructions:

1. The first thing that you will want to do is preheat your oven to 375 degrees.

2. While your oven begins to heat up make your crust. To do this stir together your first 3 ingredients together in a medium sized bowl until well mixed. Take this mixture and press it into a generously greased large sized spring form pan.

3. Place your crust into your oven to bake for the next 8 minutes. After this time remove and transfer to a wire cooling rack to cool completely.

4. Next beat your cream cheese and sugar with an electric mixer on the highest setting until light and fluffy in texture. Then add in your remaining ingredients and continue to mix until your mixture is smooth in consistency.

5. Pour this newly formed batter into your prebaked crust in your spring form pan.

6. Bake your cheesecake pan into your oven to bake for the next 15 minutes. After this time reduce the temperature of your oven to 250 degrees and continue baking for the next 50 to 55 minutes or until the cheesecake is completely set. Remove from oven and cool for at least a couple of minutes before transferring to your fridge to chill overnight, making sure that you cover the cheesecake as you do so. Serve whenever you are ready. Enjoy!

Recipe 16: Christmas Eggnog Cheesecake

This is a cheesecake recipe that I know you are going to want to prepare during the Christmas holidays. It tastes delicious, making it a cheesecake recipe that will help you and others celebrate the holiday spirit.

Yield: 16 Servings

Cooking Time: 1 Hour and 25 Minutes

List of Ingredients:

- 1 Cup of Graham Cracker, Crumbs Only
- 2 Tablespoons of Sugar, White
- 3 Tablespoons of Butter, Soft and Melted
- 3 Packs of Cream Cheese, Soft
- 1 Cup of Sugar, White
- 3 Tablespoons of Flour, All Purpose Variety
- ¾ Cup of Eggnog
- 2 Eggs, Large in Size and Beaten
- 2 Tablespoons of Rum, Your Favorite Kind
- Dash of Nutmeg, Ground

[53]

AA

Instructions:

1. The first thing that you will want to do is preheat your oven to 325 degrees. While your oven is heating up generously grease a medium sized spring form pan.

2. Then use a medium sized bowl and mix your graham cracker crumbs, butter and sugar together in a medium sized bowl until thoroughly mixed. Press this mixture into the bottom of your greased spring form pan. Place into your oven to bake for at least 10 minutes. After this time remove from oven and set on a wire cooling rack to cool thoroughly.

3. Next raise the heat of your oven to 425 degrees.

4. Then using a food processor or blender, add in your next 4 ingredients and process on the highest setting for a couple of seconds or until your mixture is smooth in consistency.

5. Add in your remaining ingredients and puree again until evenly combined and smooth in consistency.

6. Pour this mixture into your prebaked cheesecake crust.

7. Bake your cheesecake pan into your oven to bake for the next 10 minutes. Then reduce the heat of your oven to 250 degrees and continue to let your cheesecake bake for an additional 45 minutes or until your cheesecake is firm. After this time remove your cheesecake from your oven and place onto a wire cooling rack to cool completely before serving. Enjoy!

Recipe 17: Berry Packed Cheesecake

This is perhaps one of the most versatile cheesecake recipes you will ever come across. Feel free to use any kind of berries such as blueberries, cherries or raspberries in this recipe. Either way I know you are going to love it.

Yield: 10 Servings

Cooking Time: 1 Hour and 30 Minutes

Ingredients for Your Crust:

- 40 Wafers, Vanilla Flavored and Crushed
- 6 Tablespoons of Butter, Soft

Ingredients for Your Cheesecake:

- 2 Packs of Cream Cheese, Soft
- ¾ Cup of Sugar, White
- 2 Tablespoons of Flour, All Purpose Variety
- 2 teaspoons of Vanilla, Pure
- 1 Cup of Cottage Cheese, Creamed Variety
- ¼ Cup of Brandy, Cherry Flavored
- 3 Eggs, Large in Size and Beaten

Ingredients for Your Topping:

- 3 ½ Cups of Blackberries, Fresh
- 1 tablespoon of Brandy, Cherry Flavored
- 1 tablespoon of Sugar, White

Instructions:

1. The first thing that you will want to do is preheat your oven to 375 degrees. While your oven begins to heat up generously grease a medium to large sized spring form pan with a generous amount of cooking spray.

2. Then use a medium sized bowl stir together your first 2 ingredients and stir thoroughly until combined. Press this mixture into your greased spring form pan.

3. Next use a large sized bowl beat your cream cheese, all-purpose flour, pure vanilla and sugar together with an electric mixer on the highest setting until smooth in consistency. Set this mixture aside.

4. Then place your cottage cheese into a food processor and puree on the highest setting for a couple of seconds until smooth in consistency. Add in your eggs next until thoroughly combined, making sure that you do not overdo it.

5. Pour half of your newly formed cheese batter into your spring form pan followed by a layer of your fruits. Top off with your remaining cheese batter and top off with another layer of fruit.

6. Bake your cheesecake pan into your oven to bake for the next 40 to 45 minutes. Make sure that you do not overbake your cheesecake. Remove from oven and cool for at least an additional 15 minutes before transferring to a wire rack to cool completely.

7. After your cheesecake has cooled cover your cheesecake and place it into your fridge to chill for the next 4 hours.

8. While your cheesecake is chilling, make your topping. To do this combine all of your ingredients in a medium sized bowl. Once mixed cover and place into your fridge to chill for the next 2 hours. When you are ready to serve your cheesecake, top with your topping and enjoy!

Recipe 18: Cherry Packed Cheesecake

Here is yet another easy cheesecake recipe that I know you are going to want to make over and over again. It is easy to put together and tastes delicious, making this a dish that I know is going to please even the pickiest of eaters.

Yield: 12 Servings

Cooking Time: 5 Hours and 30 Minutes

List of Ingredients:

- 1 Graham Cracker Crust, Prebaked
- 1 Pack of Cream Cheese, Soft
- 1 Can of Condensed Milk, Sweetened
- 1/3 Cup of Lemon Juice, Fresh
- 1 teaspoon of Vanilla, Pure
- 1 Can of Cherry Pie, Filling Only

AAAAAAAAAAAAAAAAAAAAAAAAAAAAAAAAAAAAAAAAAAAAAA

Instructions:

1. Take out a large sized mixing bowl and combine all of your ingredients except for your cherry pie filling into it. Use an electric mixer to beat until blended thoroughly and smooth in consistency.

2. Pour this mixture into your premade pie crust.

3. Cover and set into your fridge to chill for the next 5 hours. Make sure that you do not freeze this cheesecake.

4. After this time remove your cheesecake and top with your cherry pie filling. Serve whenever you are ready and enjoy.

Recipe 19: Supreme Cheesecake

Here is yet another New York style cheesecake that you are going to fall in love with. This cheesecake is extremely filling, making it the perfect dessert dish to please even the pickiest of eaters.

Yield: 12 Servings

Cooking Time: 1 Hour and 40 Minutes

List of Ingredients:

- 1 ½ Cups of Graham Cracker, Crumbs Only
- ½ Cup of Sugar, White
- ¼ Cup of Butter, Soft
- 5 Packs of Cream Cheese, Soft
- 5 Eggs, Large in Size and Beaten
- 2 Eggs, Yolks Only
- 1 ¾ Cups of Sugar, White
- 1/8 Cup of Flour, All Purpose Variety
- ¼ Cup of Heavy Cream, Whipping Variety

AAAAAAAAAAAAAAAAAAAAAAAAAAAAAAAAAAAAAAAAAAAAA

Instructions:

1. The first thing that you will want to do is preheat your oven to 400 degrees. While your oven begins to heat up generously grease a medium to large sized spring form pan with a generous amount of cooking spray.

2. Take your first 3 ingredients together and mix thoroughly until mixed extremely well. Press this mixture into your greased spring form pan.

3. Next beat your next 3 ingredients with an electric mixer on the highest setting until smooth in consistency. Add in your remaining ingredients and continue to mix until your mixture is smooth in consistency.

4. Pour this newly formed batter into your greased spring form pan.

5. Bake your cheesecake pan into your oven to bake for the next 10 minutes before turning down the temperature of your oven to 200 degrees. Continue baking for at least 1 hour or until your cheesecake is fully set. Remove from oven and cool for at least a couple of minutes before transferring to your fridge to chill for an hour or so. Serve whenever you are ready and enjoy!

Recipe 20: Tasty Tiramisu Cheesecake

This is one tasty cheesecake recipe that I know you will be dying to make. This cheesecake incorporates the deliciousness of Tiramisu and New York style cheesecake, making it a cheesecake dish that is packed full of flavor.

Yield: 12 Servings

Cooking Time: 5 Hours

List of Ingredients:

- 1 Pack of Ladyfingers, Prepackaged
- 4 Tablespoons of Butter, Soft and Melted
- 4 Tablespoons of Coffee, Liquored Variety
- 3 Packs of Cream Cheese, Soft
- 1 Container of Cheese, Mascarpone Variety
- 1 Cup of Sugar, White
- 2 Eggs, Large in Size and Beaten
- 4 Tablespoons of Flour, All Purpose Variety
- 1 Square of Chocolate, Semisweet Variety

AAAAAAAAAAAAAAAAAAAAAAAAAAAAAAAAAAAAAAAAAAAAAA

Instructions:

1. The first thing that you will want to do is preheat your oven to 350 degrees. While your oven is heating up take out a large sized pan and fill it with water. Place into the bottom of your oven.

2. Next take your ladyfingers and crush them until you have finely crushed crumbs left. Mix your soft and melted butter with these crumbs and stir until thoroughly mixed together. Add about 2 tablespoon of your liqueur and stir again to incorporate. Press this mixture into a large sized spring form pan and set aside.

3. The next step is to use a large sized mixing bowl and mix together your cream cheese, mascarpone cheese and sugar. Beat this mixture with an electric mixer until smooth in consistency. Add in your remaining ingredients except for your semisweet chocolate, making sure to beat it vigorously until evenly combined.

4. Next pour your batter into your already made cheesecake crust.

5. Bake your cheesecake pan into your oven to bake for the next 40 to 45 minutes or until fully set. After this time turn off your oven and open the door, allowing your cheesecake to cool for about 20 minutes. After this time remove from heat and place into your fridge to chill for at least 3 hours or overnight if you can.

6. Right before you are ready to serve, finely grate your chocolate over the top as a garnish. Serve and enjoy!

Recipe 21: Mini Cheesecakes

These little cheesecakes are the best little snack to make especially if you want to treat a bunch of people to something special. Feel free to make this dish for any kind of upcoming holiday or special occasion.

Yield: 48 Servings

Cooking Time: 45 Minutes

List of Ingredients:

- 1 Pack of Wafers, Vanilla Flavored
- 2 Packs of Cream Cheese, Soft
- ¾ Cup of Sugar, White
- 2 Eggs, Large in Size and Beaten
- 1 teaspoon of Vanilla, Pure
- 1 Can of Cherry Pie, Filling and Canned

AAAAAAAAAAAAAAAAAAAAAAAAAAAAAAAAAAAAAAAAAAAAA

Instructions:

1. The first thing that you will want to do is preheat your oven to 350 degrees. While your oven begins to heat up generously grease a medium to large sized miniature muffin pan with a generous amount of cooking spray or muffin liners.

2. Next crush up your vanilla flavored wafers and place at least ½ teaspoon or more into the bottom of your miniature muffin cups.

3. Then beat the rest of your ingredients except for your cherry pie filling with an electric mixer on the highest setting until smooth and fluffy in consistency.

4. Pour this newly formed batter into your miniature muffin cups, making sure to fill them at least ¾ of the way full.

5. Bake in your oven for the next 15 minutes or until fully set. Remove from oven and cool for at least a couple of minutes. Top with at least 1 teaspoon of your cherry pie filling and serve whenever you are ready.

Recipe 22: Cookie Crumb Cheesecake

This is one cheesecake recipe that I know you will become addicted to. It is extremely decadent and one of the best dessert dishes that you will ever have the pleasure to make.

Yield: 14 Servings

Cooking Time: 11 Hours

List of Ingredients:

- 2 Cups of Cookie Crumbs, Chocolate Sandwich Variety
- 2 Tablespoons of Butter, Soft and Melted
- ¼ Cup of Brown Sugar, Light and Packed
- 1 teaspoon of Cinnamon, Ground
- 2 Pounds of Cream Cheese, Soft
- 1 ¼ Cups of Sugar, White
- 1/3 Cup of Whipping Cream, Heavy Variety
- 2 Tablespoons of Flour, All Purpose Variety
- 1 teaspoon of Vanilla, Pure
- 4 Eggs, Large in Size and Beaten
- 1 ½ Cups of Cookie Crumbs, Chocolate Sandwich Variety
- 16 Ounces of Sour Cream
- ¼ Cup of Sugar, White
- 1 teaspoon of Vanilla, Pure
- 1 Cup of Whipping Cream, Heavy Variety
- 1 ½ Cups of Chocolate Chips, Semisweet Variety
- 1 teaspoon of Vanilla, Pure

AAAAAAAAAAAAAAAAAAAAAAAAAAAAAAAAAAAAAAAAAAAA

Instructions:

1. The first thing that you will want to do is preheat your oven to 325 degrees. While your oven is heating up generously grease a large sized spring form pan.

2. Then use a medium sized bowl and mix together your first 4 ingredients together in a medium sized bowl until thoroughly mixed. Press this mixture into the bottom of your greased spring form pan. Place into your oven to bake for at least 5 to 10 minutes. After this time remove from oven and set aside to cool.

3. Next use a large sized bowl and beat together your cream cheese with an electric mixer until smooth in consistency. Then add in your next 5 ingredients and continue to beat until your batter is smooth in consistency.

4. Pour at least 1/3 of your prepared batter into your prebaked cheesecake crust. Top off with your cookie crumbs. Pour in your remaining cheesecake batter.

5. Bake your cheesecake pan into your oven to bake for the next 45 minutes or until fully set. After this time remove your cheesecake from your oven and set aside.

6. While your cheesecake is baking combine your sugar, pure vanilla and sour cream together until thoroughly combined. Pour this over your baked cheesecake. Return to your oven and continue to bake for an additional 7 minutes. After this time turn off your oven and allow your cheesecake to sit inside for at least 30 more minutes. After this time remove from oven and set on a wire cooling rack to cool completely.

7. While your cheesecake cooling combine the rest of your ingredients in a small sized sauce pan and heat until your chocolate completely melts. Stir until thoroughly combine. Remove from heat.

8. Pour your chocolate mixture over your cheesecake and cover. Place into your fridge for at least 8 hours and serve whenever you are ready.

Recipe 23: Autumn Style Cheesecake

This is perhaps the best cheesecake to make right at the beginning of the fall season. It is also great to make to bring in the Thanksgiving holiday. It is absolutely delicious and every easy to make. I know you will love it.

Yield: 12 Servings

Cooking Time: 4 Hours

Ingredients for Your Crust:

- 1 Cup of Graham Crackers, Crumbs Only
- ½ Cup of Pecans, Chopped Finely
- 3 Tablespoons of Sugar, White
- ½ teaspoons of Cinnamon, Ground
- ¼ Cup of Butter, Unsalted and Melted

Ingredients for Your Filling:

- 2 Packs of Cream Cheese, Soft
- ½ Cup of Sugar, White
- 2 Eggs, Large in Size and Beaten

Ingredients for Topping:

- ½ teaspoons of Vanilla, Pure
- 4 Cups of Apples, Peeled, Cored and Sliced
- 1/3 Cup of Sugar, White
- ½ teaspoons of Cinnamon Ground
- ¼ Cup of Pecans, Finely Chopped

AAAAAAAAAAAAAAAAAAAAAAAAAAAAAAAAAAAAAAAAAAAAA

Instructions:

1. The first thing that you will want to do is preheat your oven to 350 degrees. While your oven is heating up generously grease a medium sized spring form pan.

2. Then mix together your first 5 ingredients together in a medium sized bowl until thoroughly mixed. Press this mixture into the bottom of your greased spring form pan. Place into your oven to bake for at least 10 hours. After this time remove and allow to cool.

3. Next beat your cream cheese and cottage cheese with an electric mixer on the highest setting until light and fluffy in texture. Then add in your remaining filling ingredients together, making sure that you mix vigorously until thoroughly combined.

4. Pour this newly formed batter into your spring form pan.

5. Then use a small sized bowl and stir together your topping ingredients except for your pecans until thoroughly coated. Pour this mixture on top of your cream cheese mixture in your pan. Garnish with a thin layer of finely chopped pecans.

6. Bake your cheesecake pan into your oven to bake for the next 60 to 70 minutes. Make sure that you do not overbake your cheesecake. After this time remove your cheesecake from your oven and allow to chill in your fridge before serving.

Recipe 24: Marble Style Pumpkin Cheesecake

This is yet another great tasting pumpkin cheesecake made with a mouthwatering gingerbread crust that will leave you craving for more. This is one dish that you can make during the fall holiday season to make a tasty treat for everybody to enjoy.

Yield: 12 Servings

Cooking Time: 7 Hours and 40 Minutes

List of Ingredients:

- 1 ½ Cups of Gingersnap Cookies, Finely Crushed
- ½ Cup of Pecans, Finely Chopped
- 1/3 Cup of Butter, Soft and Melted
- 2 Packs of Cream Cheese, Soft
- ¾ Cup of Sugar, White and Evenly Divided
- 1 teaspoon of Vanilla, Pure
- 3 Eggs, Large in Size and Beaten
- 1 Cup of Pumpkin, Canned and Puree
- ¾ teaspoons of Cinnamon, Ground
- ¼ teaspoons of Nutmeg, Ground

AAAAAAAAAAAAAAAAAAAAAAAAAAAAAAAAAAAAAAAAAAAA

Instructions:

1. The first thing that you will want to do is preheat your oven to 350 degrees. While your oven is heating up generously grease a medium sized spring form pan.

2. Then use a medium sized bowl and mix together your first 3 ingredients together in a medium sized bowl until thoroughly mixed. Press this mixture into the bottom of your greased spring form pan. Place into your preheated oven and bake for the next 10 minutes. After this time remove from oven and set aside for later use.

3. Next use a medium sized bowl and add in your cream cheese, sugar and pure vanilla. Mix together with an electric mixer until smooth in consistency. Spoon at least 1 cup of this mixture out and set aside.

4. Then add in your remaining and ingredients into your remaining batter and continue to beat until evenly mixed together.

5. Next melt your chocolate chips until completely melted. Combine with your half and half and stir continuously until your mixture is smooth in consistency.

6. Next pour your pumpkin cheesecake batter into your spring form batter then add in your plain batter on the top. Use a knife to swirl the plain batter around on the top of your cheesecake to give it a marble look.

7. Place your cheesecake into your oven and bake for the next 55 minutes or until fully set. After this time remove your cheesecake from your oven, cover and allow to chill in your fridge for the next 4 hours before serving.

Recipe 25: White Chocolate Cheesecake

If you are a huge fan of white chocolate like I am, then I know for certain that you are going to fall in love with this recipe. This dish is a perfect dessert treat to serve for nearly any occasion and I guarantee that your guests will love it as well.

Yield: 16 Servings

Cooking Time: 10 Hours

List of Ingredients:

- 1 Cup of Cookies, Chocolate Variety and Crumbs Only
- 3 Tablespoons of Sugar, White
- ¼ Cup of Butter, Soft
- 1 Pack of Raspberries, Frozen and Thawed
- 2 Tablespoons of Sugar, White
- 2 teaspoons of Cornstarch
- 1/2 Cup of Water
- 2 Cups of Chocolate Chips, White Variety
- ½ Cup of Half-and-Half
- 3 Packs of Cream Cheese, Soft
- ½ Cup of Sugar, White
- 3 Eggs, Large in Size and Beaten
- 1 teaspoon of Vanilla, Pure

Instructions:

1. The first thing that you will want to do is preheat your oven to 325 degrees. While your oven is heating up generously grease a medium sized spring form pan.

2. Then use a medium sized bowl and mix together your first 3 ingredients together in a medium sized bowl until thoroughly mixed. Press this mixture into the bottom of your greased spring form pan. Set aside.

3. Next use a large sized saucepan, add in your next 4 ingredients and stir together until thoroughly combined. Bring this mixture over medium heat and heat up until you bring it to a boil. Allow to boil for at least 5 minutes or until your sauce is thick in consistency. Once thick remove from heat and strain this sauce through a fine strainer.

4. Next melt your chocolate chips until completely melted. Combine with your half and half and stir continuously until your mixture is smooth in consistency.

5. The next step is to use a large sized mixing bowl and mix together your cream cheese and sugar. Beat this mixture with an electric mixer until smooth in consistency. Add in your eggs, pure vanilla and melted chocolate, beating vigorously until evenly combined.

6. Next pour your cheesecake batter into your spring form batter then add in at least 3 tablespoons of your raspberry mixture on top of your cheesecake batter. Add some more of your cheesecake batter followed by a top of your raspberry mixture.

7. Bake your cheesecake pan into your oven to bake for the next 55 to 60 minutes or until fully set. After this time remove your cheesecake from your oven, cover and allow to chill in your fridge before serving.

About the Author

Molly Mills always knew she wanted to feed people delicious food for a living. Being the oldest child with three younger brothers, Molly learned to prepare meals at an early age to help out her busy parents. She just seemed to know what spice went with which meat and how to make sauces that would dress up the blandest of pastas. Her creativity in the kitchen was a blessing to a family where money was tight and making new meals every day was a challenge.

Molly was also a gifted athlete as well as chef and secured a Lacrosse scholarship to Syracuse University. This was a blessing to her family as she was the first to go to college and at little cost to her parents. She took full advantage of her college education and earned a business degree. When she graduated, she joined her culinary skills and business acumen into a successful catering business. She wrote her first e-book after a customer asked if she could pay for several of her recipes. This sparked the entrepreneurial spirit in Mills and she thought if one person wanted them, then why not share the recipes with the world!

Molly lives near her family's home with her husband and three children and still cooks for her family every chance she gets. She plays Lacrosse with a local team made up of her old teammates from college and there are always some tasty nibbles on the ready after each game.

Don't Miss Out!

Scan the QR-Code below and you can sign up to receive emails whenever Molly Mills publishes a new book. There's no charge and no obligation.

Sign Me Up

https://molly.gr8.com

Printed in Great Britain
by Amazon

35355450R00051